WORKBOOK 5

prepared for the course team by margaret kiloh

This publication forms part of an Open University course DD100 *An Introduction to the Social Sciences: Understanding Social Change*. Details of this and other Open University courses can be obtained from the Call Centre, PO Box 724, The Open University, Milton Keynes MK7 6ZS, United Kingdom: tel. +44 (0)1908 653231, e-mail ces-gen@open.ac.uk

Alternatively, you may visit the Open University website at http://www.open.ac.uk where you can learn more about the wide range of courses and packs offered at all levels by The Open University.

To purchase this publication or other components of Open University courses, contact Open University Worldwide Ltd, The Berrill Building, Walton Hall, Milton Keynes MK7 6AA, United Kingdom: tel. +44 (0)1908 858785; fax +44 (0)1908 858787; e-mail ouwenq@open.ac.uk; website http://www.ouw.co.uk

The Open University
Walton Hall, Milton Keynes
MK7 6AA

First published 2000. Second edition 2001

Edited, designed and typeset by The Open University.

Printed in the United Kingdom by The Bath Press, Bath.

ISBN 0 7492 7738 6

2.1

20305B/dd100wb5i2.1

Contents

The DD100 course team

John Allen, *Senior Lecturer in Geography*

Penny Bennett, *Editor*

Pam Berry, *Compositor*

Simon Bromley, *Senior Lecturer in Government*

David Calderwood, *Project Controller*

Elizabeth Chaplin, *Tutor Panel*

Giles Clark, *Co-publishing Advisor*

Stephen Clift, *Editor*

Allan Cochrane, *Professor of Public Policy*

Lene Connolly, *Print Buying Controller*

Graham Dawson, *Lecturer in Economics*

Lesley Duguid, *Senior Course Co-ordination Secretary*

Fran Ford, *Senior Course Co-ordination Secretary*

David Goldblatt, *Co-Course Team Chair, Lecturer in Government*

Jenny Gove, *Lecturer in Psychology*

Judith Greene, *Professor of Psychology*

Montserrat Guibernau, *Lecturer in Government*

Peter Hamilton, *Lecturer in Sociology*

Celia Hart, *Picture Researcher*

David Held, *Professor of Politics and Sociology*

Susan Himmelweit, *Senior Lecturer in Economics*

Steve Hinchliffe, *Lecturer in Geography*

Anne Howells, *Project Controller*

Gordon Hughes, *Lecturer in Social Policy*

Christina Janoszka, *Course Manager*

Pat Jess, *Staff Tutor in Geography (Region 12)*

Bob Kelly, *Staff Tutor in Government (Region 06)*

Margaret Kiloh, *Staff Tutor in Applied Social Sciences (Region 13)*

Sylvia Lay-Flurrie, *Secretary*

Siân Lewis, *Graphic Designer*

Tony McGrew, *Professor of International Relations, University of Southampton*

Hugh Mackay, *Staff Tutor in Sociology (Region 10)*

Maureen Mackintosh, *Professor of Economics*

Eugene McLaughlin, *Senior Lecturer in Applied Social Science*

Andrew Metcalf, *Senior Producer, BBC*

Gerry Mooney, *Staff Tutor in Applied Social Sciences (Region 11)*

Ray Munns, *Graphic Artist*

Kathy Pain, *Staff Tutor in Geography (Region 02)*

Clive Pearson, *Tutor Panel*

Lynne Poole, *Tutor Panel*

Norma Sherratt, *Staff Tutor in Sociology (Region 03)*

Roberto Simonetti, *Lecturer in Economics*

Dick Skellington, *Project Officer*

Brenda Smith, *Staff Tutor in Psychology (Region 12)*

Mark Smith, *Lecturer in Social Sciences*

Grahame Thompson, *Professor of Political Economy*

Ken Thompson, *Professor of Sociology*

Stuart Watt, *Lecturer in Psychology/KMI*

Andy Whitehead, *Graphic Artist*

Kath Woodward, *Co-Course Team Chair, Staff Tutor in Sociology (Region 07)*

Chris Wooldridge, *Editor*

External Assessor

Nigel Thrift, *Professor of Geography, University of Bristol*

INTRODUCTION

Welcome to Block 5. You are now almost on the last lap of your course so you are well acquainted with the formula for these workbooks. You know that they are not prescriptive but we hope that by now you have found that they are really useful in helping you to allocate your time, to work through the materials for the block and to practice essential study skills. As the rest of the summer looms ahead you may need extra help in keeping to the straight and narrow path of studying social science. The explanations and exercises in this workbook are geared to do that and to help you with your preparation for TMA 05 at the end of the block. Enjoy the summer – but keep up the good work!

Block overview

The theme of Block 5, *Knowledge and the Social Sciences*, provides the key to all of your further study in the social sciences, no matter what you decide to do next year. Even if you decide to go on to study in another faculty or not to register for another course you should leave the block with a thorough understanding of how the social sciences work and how they compare with other subjects, which will be of enormous value to you in simply looking at life.

The various components of the block and the recommended route through them are shown in Figures 1 and 2 (overleaf).

Study week	Course material	Suggested study time
26	*Workbook 5* and Book 5: *Knowledge and the Social Sciences: Theory, Method, Practice* Introduction Chapter 1 Audio-cassette 9, Side A and notes	12 hours
27	Workbook and Chapter 2	12 hours
28	Workbook and Chapter 3	12 hours
29	Workbook, Chapter 4 and Afterword Audio-cassette 9, Side B and notes TV 05 and notes	12 hours
30	Workbook and TMA 05	12 hours

FIGURE 1   Course materials for Block 5

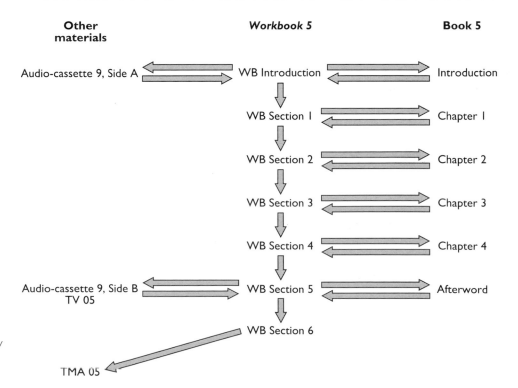

FIGURE 2
Recommended study route for Block 5

It won't have escaped your attention that this block is directly concerned with one of the course themes – *knowledge and knowing*. As both the *Introductory Workbook* (p.36) and the *Mid Course Review* (pp.33–4) pointed out, this has a narrative and an analytical aspect. The analytical strand uses the *circuit of knowledge* to examine the process by which we come to say that we 'know' something. The narrative strand explores the nature of 'knowledge' itself, how there are different kinds of knowledge and how our beliefs about the way the world is structured are not constant but are constantly changing.

 Now please read the Introduction to Book 5, *Knowledge and the Social Sciences: Theory, Method, Practice*, listen to Audio-cassette 9, Side A, and read the associated notes. Then return to this point in the workbook.

Knowledge and knowing: narrative strand

In Block 5 the narrative strand is structured by a number of key questions which are outlined in the Introduction to Book 5.

Key questions

1   What is knowledge?

Block 5 is concerned first of all with the nature of knowledge, what different kinds of knowledge there are and what the social sources and significance of these might be. Philosophers, priests, scientists and, finally, social scientists have long been preoccupied by the question, what is knowledge? Frustratingly, each has come up with a very different answer!

When social scientists look at knowledge they try to go beyond the simple dictionary definition and to 'unpack' all of the different ways in which we use this concept. As the Introduction to Book 5 points out, knowledge is not just 'an organized body of information' (Oxford English Dictionary). It can also be a body of skills, ideas, practices and ways of understanding the world.

If you think about it, there are many different kinds of knowledge. These include religious knowledge, natural scientific knowledge, and social scientific knowledge but we expect you can think of others too. We think you would agree that the ones we have listed are clearly quite different things. But to understand the nature of knowledge we need to ask why this is so. What is it that makes them different from one another?

2   How is knowledge socially constructed?

Different societies produce different kinds of knowledge and knowledge is not static. For example, medical knowledge in the past was almost completely different to medical knowledge today. Until the gradual acceptance of Darwin's theory of evolution people 'knew' that the story of Genesis was literally true and even nowadays Western and Eastern systems of thought lead to very different interpretations and explanations of events.

Each society has institutions and structures that influence the kind of knowledge that is seen as legitimate. These are closely connected with the way that power is distributed in society and the way that this is reflected in language and discourse. Indeed, the ability to control knowledge and ideas is one of the most important weapons at the disposal of those who hold power. Galileo was imprisoned because his contention that the earth revolved around the sun undermined the power of the scientific and religious establishment of the day. In sixteenth-century France, where power was exercised by an absolute monarch and a hereditary aristocracy, the belief system that operated supported the idea of the divine right of kings and the classifications of the feudal system, keeping the majority of the population in misery. Nowadays France is a republic and even monarchists would not subscribe to a belief in divine right.

This is what we mean when we say that all knowledge is socially constructed or *socially produced*.

3   Has there been a decline in trust in expert knowledge?

Some social scientists have argued that a key aspect of society at the beginning of the new millennium is an increase in diversity both within and between different knowledge systems and a consequent increase in uncertainty and decline in trust of experts who purport to convey universal truths. It is certainly true that the increasing complexity of problems has led to a search for new answers, which may challenge natural scientific, political or religious orthodoxy. At the same time there has been a freeing up of knowledge and alternative forms of knowledge are now available to many through the rapid growth of communication technology.

The power of traditional experts, which rested on the monopolization and control of knowledge, has indeed been diminished, but we should not exaggerate either the amount of certainty which existed before or the extent to which belief in expert power has been overturned. Institutions and structures are slow to change and the old expert elites still have considerable power.

Paradoxically, it could be argued, the democratization and spread of knowledge through globalization, the development of the natural sciences and medical advance has not brought about a decline in trust of experts in general so much as a search for new 'gurus' to provide explanations, legitimacy and certainty. There has been a rise in extreme forms of nationalism and fundamentalist religions and a proliferation of alternative therapies and beliefs.

WORKBOOK ACTIVITY I

As a social scientist you need to be able to look at different sides of any question. Practice this by thinking of one example to back up the argument that there *has* been a decrease in trust in expert knowledge and one example to back up the argument that there has not.

For:

Against:

COMMENT _____

There are lots of possible examples that you might use here. An example of the decline in trust (one close to our own hearts!) might be the decline in the status and pay of the teaching profession. On the other hand, most of us do still take the word of a hospital consultant, and the newspapers and television seem to be full of experts and pundits to whom we give credence, so maybe the 'democratization' of knowledge has been exaggerated.

Remember, there is always more than one side to any question and when assessing any form of argument it is important to be aware of the values and purpose which lie behind that argument. Later on we will be looking again at this issue and at ways of *evaluating* different answers and proofs.

4   Can knowledge produce social change?

Knowledge can produce social change in a number of different ways. As we have noted above, challenges to accepted knowledge and received wisdom frequently have a profound effect, resulting in the overthrow of established systems of knowledge and power. This process may be gradual and evolutionary but it may also be the result of the organization and deployment of knowledge and ideas for the specific purpose of bringing about change.

Despite the popular image of scholars in their ivory towers dedicating their lives to the love of knowledge, knowledge is rarely acquired for its own sake. For example, doctors want to understand the human body so that they can cure illness; monks shut themselves up in mediaeval libraries so that they could acquire the key to salvation and when Machiavelli (the Florentine philosopher whose name became an English adjective) wrote his sixteenth-century manual of statecraft, *The Prince*, it was so that he and his prospective master could hold on to the reins of power. Social scientists, by and large, study society not just to understand it but because they want to be able to predict developments. And some study social change so as to be able to influence the direction of that change and to prescribe future action that will lead to a particular result. For them the objective is quite simple – they want to change the world!

One of the points which we have been hammering home throughout this course is that social science knowledge (like natural science knowledge) is organized through *theories* – arguments about how things work and how they interact. As you know, there are many competing theories and these are open to debate, testable and changeable in the light of different evidence. As *Workbook 4*, Section 2.4 pointed out, the relationship between theory and ideology is a complex one. Some theories, like those of Karl Marx, may be taken up, developed and organized in the form of *ideologies* (like Marxism) that aim not just to describe and explain the way things are but also to prescribe the way that things *should* be. Alternatively, theories may be heavily influenced and shaped by existing political ideologies. Unlike theories, ideologies tend to be closed systems of knowledge and they may have a revolutionary impact on social change.

Knowledge and knowing: analytical strand

As well as exploring new aspects of the knowledge and knowing narrative this block completes the analytical strand of the theme by looking at the *theory* of knowledge and knowing (known as *epistemology*) and at the key question of how we 'know' something.

One of the things which the narrative strand of the block demonstrates is that different forms of knowledge use different kinds of evidence or proof to substantiate themselves. The philosopher Descartes famously proved his own existence to himself with the conclusion 'I think, therefore I am'. Doctors, religious believers, economists or psychologists look for different kinds of proof.

WORKBOOK ACTIVITY 2

Take a minute to think about the kind of proof that a doctor might consider to be convincing and compare that with the kind of proof that religious believers would accept.

COMMENT _____

Doctors perform operations or prescribe medicines because they believe that they know the cause of an illness and how to cure it. This knowledge is endorsed by the medical establishment and generally accepted by the population at large. The 'proof' of their knowledge (what we have called 'verification') is the repeated success of their treatments and the recovery of their patients – a painkiller is taken and the pain goes away so this proves that they are right. Religious believers believe that they know that God exists and they also see 'proof' of this in a variety of ways. Some look to the experts of the religious establishment such as priests and bishops, some look for literal truth in the bible, some look for evidence of the power of prayer, some believe in miracles and for some life itself is sufficient proof.

What counts as proof in one context is not necessarily acceptable in another. The examples which you will have thought of will all be specific to the here and now. If you had been answering at another time or in another place or culture your examples might have been very different. Early medicine was based on a combination of spells and herbalism and, as Chapter 1 points out, for the ancient Greeks illness and health were ascribed to the balance of different 'humours' in the body. Similarly, in China today there is a whole different system of medicine based on acupuncture and pressure points. These differences are not just variations on the same thing but stem from the fact that all forms of knowledge are part and parcel of the society in which they are situated and they are affected by that society.

Because all forms of knowledge are open to doubt, the social sciences use what we have called the circuit of knowledge as a way of developing, testing and verifying explanations and evidence about society. The blocks so far have dealt with the way in which social scientists:

- begin with questions
- turn them into testable, clear hypotheses, descriptive statements, or explanatory models or theories
- seek out, organize and evaluate evidence
- apply the evidence to the original hypothesis/statement/explanation/ theory
- evaluate the theory confirming, refuting, or modifying it.

The workbooks so far have 'unpacked' for you how social scientists construct arguments (Block 1), use evidence (Block 2), develop theories (Block 3), and how social scientists evaluate theories and evidence (Block 4). The final step in this process, which we will be dealing with in this workbook, is the synthesis

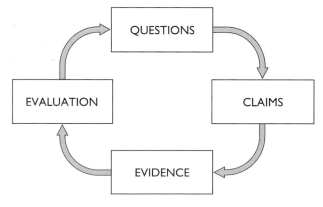

FIGURE 3   The circuit of knowledge

and integration of all the information and evidence (including 'failed' theories) and the generation of a new set of questions, hypotheses and theories.

Key skills

We expect that by the end of this block you will have built on the skill of assessing and comparing evidence and theories with which you became familiar in *Workbook 4* and will have had further practice in evaluating arguments and explanations. You will also have been shown how to synthesize information and theories and integrate them into a coherent whole. Put like that it sounds terribly difficult, so let's explore what we mean.

You might wonder why we are talking about synthesis and integration as separate skills. The dictionary definitions of the two words are virtually identical and in everyday language they are often used interchangeably. There are, however, two separate processes involved here:

- *bringing together* different theories, concepts and evidence (synthesizing), and
- *combining* them into something new (integrating).

Think of it like making a cake – you bring together the various ingredients and transform them to make something which is the sum of those ingredients but also something completely different.

Making a cake

In the same way that you can learn to make a cake you can learn how to use synthesis and integrate information and theories. Don't worry if you don't turn into Delia Smith overnight! We will be illustrating how to go about it with activities and questions to help you as we go through the chapters and we are confident that as you near Block 6 you really will have acquired a tremendous amount of new skills:

- You will be adopting a much more critical approach to arguments and be able to assess them.

- You will be pulling together material from different parts of the course.

- You will have stopped accepting what the authors of the chapters say (if you ever did!) and we will have achieved our objective of turning you into if not a fully-fledged social scientist at least one ready to leave the nest and learn to fly.

Assessing Block 5

The best way of learning to fly is by practising and this is what TMA 05 has been designed to encourage you to do. The assignment for this block consists of a 1,500 word essay which will require you to draw on more than one of the chapters in Book 5. This is designed to test both your knowledge and understanding of the course material and your skill in bringing together and integrating different theories and evidence. The workbook is structured so as to help you first to break down and evaluate the arguments which are presented into their component parts and then to practice the skill of drawing on these to put together your own argument. Towards the end of the workbook you will be asked to work through a similar question step by step in preparation for the TMA itself.

Reflective learning

Throughout this course you have been encouraged to reflect on your own learning, including the feedback on your TMAs. Reflective learning means thinking about what you have done so far, identifying your own strengths and weaknesses, and taking any lessons that you have learned to help you with what is to come. At this time of the year you can put this to some direct use. On the practical front, August is a month when there are likely to be interruptions to your study routine (children at home, annual holidays, etc.). There is also less study support available because most tutorials are suspended until September. Before plunging into Block 5 it is worth looking ahead and pausing to ask yourself a few questions.

- How am I going to cope with changes in routine or location? (That is, when and where am I going to study?)

- Are there any fellow students I can meet up with to help keep me going through the summer?

- Are there any conceptual difficulties or study problems that I need to discuss with my tutor-counsellor before he or she disappears on holiday?

You may need to reschedule your work to take account of domestic or work difficulties. If so, *tell your tutor-counsellor* and work out a strategy for dealing with it.

After Block 5 you will be working with the *End of Course Review* and your final TMA which draws on the whole of the course, so the end of this block would be a good time to look back, to identify any gaps in your study which you may have been forced to make and to discuss with your tutor-counsellor how you are going to tackle the review block.

1 SCIENCE AND SOCIETY: KNOWLEDGE IN MEDICINE

As we noted in the *Introductory Workbook* (p.36), 'all forms of knowledge, be they common sense, the natural sciences or the social sciences, are open to doubt'. Our apparent sense of certainty rested on the idea that there were certain truths about the world and that 'experts' could be relied upon to interpret these accurately and to provide reliable information for us. But was this ever really true? Or is it simply that some forms of knowledge, both then and now, are privileged over others by virtue of the power and authority of these expert agents? To what extent is knowledge in reality structured by society?

Chapter 1 uses the narrative of the development of medical knowledge and the medical profession to argue that knowledge and knowing are the product of *social institutions*, not some independent intellectual source. Looked at in terms of structure and agency, there is a tension between individual agency and structure in knowledge. Experts are not free agents. They derive their legitimacy from knowledge-structures already embedded in society and as society changes knowledge and knowing change with it. Nevertheless, new ideas have an important role to play in bringing about social change.

KEY TASKS

Chapter 1, 'Science and Society. Knowledge in Medicine'.

- To identify the main argument of the chapter and separate this from the illustrations used.

- To understand what the chapter has to say about the social production of knowledge, the role of experts, and the role of language.

- To be able to compare the development of natural scientific and social scientific methods.

- To relate the chapter to the other course themes of *structure and agency* and *uncertainty and diversity*.

Now please read Chapter 1, 'Science and Society: Knowledge in Medicine', and then return to this point in the workbook.

1.1 Narrative strand: the social production of knowledge

At first glance Chapter 1 might seem to be 'about' medicine, but appearances can be deceptive. In reality the chapter uses the example of medicine merely as an illustration of natural scientific knowledge in order to explore the relationship between science and society, 'the social production of knowledge and the diversity of knowledge systems' (p.10).

1.1.1 Identifying the argument

Although this chapter contains a lot of information about medicine this 'story line' is used primarily to illustrate a much broader argument. What we want you to get out of the chapter is <u>not</u> a detailed knowledge of the nature of medical science – so there is no point in taking copious notes on the subject! Our objective is for you to understand the argument of the chapter and to be able to distinguish that from the supporting medical examples. The first step is for you to identify the broad argument which runs through the chapter.

WORKBOOK ACTIVITY 1.1

Drawing on what you have learned about note-taking techniques from previous workbooks, choose a quick way of identifying the main points of the argument in each section of Chapter 1 and jot down no more than six points for each section in your own words. (If you absolutely can't think of any other way to say it put quotation marks round it, and make a note of the page reference.)

COMMENT

Previous workbooks have suggested a number of techniques including looking at the book's Introduction, looking at the chapter's contents list, looking at the chapter introduction and conclusion, and looking at the summaries. A single technique isn't always appropriate. On this occasion the book's Introduction is a bit too general and the headings and sub-headings in the chapter could reinforce the impression that the argument is mainly about medicine. On the other hand, the chapter's introduction, conclusion and summaries are really useful.

Note that the summary at the end of Chapter 1 (p.38), whilst still using the example of medicine, provides the basis of the argument which is about knowledge in general and more specifically scientific knowledge. This is (still using mainly the original wording of the chapter):

- There are whole ranges of different systems of knowledge.

- Knowledge is produced in particular circumstances at particular times; it is historically specific.

- Scientific knowledge is characterized by specialized language which defines and delimits what is included and what is excluded.

- New ideas and language are created in response to what has gone before; existing discourses are challenged by new systems of knowledge.

- There are different, both competing and complementary, sets of knowledge which we draw on to define and explain phenomena.

- There are challenges to traditional authority and expertise and the proliferation of different ideas which can create uncertainty as well as diversity.

The Chapter 1 authors have summed this up so neatly, haven't they? But what we want is not *their* understanding but *yours*. If you just copy down what they say, and then later on reproduce it in an assignment, there is no evidence that you have really *understood* the argument. If you translate it into your own words then you will own it – and you will internalize it much more easily.

For example, instead of the penultimate point ('There are different, both competing and complementary, sets of knowledge which we draw on to define and explain phenomena'). We could say 'Whenever we are trying to understand and explain things there is more than one source of knowledge available to us. Some of these sources may contradict each other, others may agree and provide additional information or approaches.' More long-winded perhaps but it spells out what *we* think the authors are saying, rather than simply repeating their original words.

1.1.2 Arguments and examples

One of the key points which is identified above is the argument that knowledge is not 'given' or self-evident but is 'produced' by reference to different kinds of evidence. The next stage in unpicking the argument of the chapter involves separating the development of this argument from the examples which are used to illustrate it. One way of doing this is to build up a grid for each section identifying the main points in the argument on one side and the examples on the other. We have done this below for Section 1.

Argument	Examples/evidence
There are different sources of knowledge	Medical knowledge:
	(a) qualitative – personal experience (e.g. cough)
	(b) quantitative – scientific evidence (e.g. blood pressure and temperature)
	(c) expert – professional experience and training (e.g. doctors).
Knowledge is 'socially produced'	Ideas about illness may depend on:
	(a) popular culture (e.g. relating to stress)
	(b) common sense (e.g. comments from friends)
	(c) alternative belief systems (e.g. holistic medicine)
	(d) 'socially sanctioned' expertise (e.g. GPs).
Expert knowledge has a superior status and authority and is socially sanctioned	Doctors are permitted to prescribe drugs and perform operations.
	Employers accept a medical certificate as a valid proof of illness.
Expert knowledge has a specialized language and methodology that helps to keep it apart from common sense and to create new knowledge	The working of the body, illness and drugs are described and categorized using a specialized language (Latin or Greek).
	Doctors use observations and instruments to test and assess evidence and diagnose illness.

In filling in the grid we were careful to do two things. First, as far as the argument column was concerned, we separated the general argument of the chapter from any *specific* argument about medicine. Second, in the examples/evidence column, we didn't just list all of the detailed examples; we tried to *group* them in a useful way which might help with any later analysis of the argument (e.g. as 'qualitative', 'quantitative', 'expert', 'popular culture', 'common sense', 'alternative') and to give just one example for each category.

WORKBOOK ACTIVITY 1.2

Re-read the rest of the chapter then have a go at completing the grid below. Fill in the steps in the argument on the left-hand side of the grid and the examples used on the right. Note that the argument is not always directly stated in a single sentence. You may need to draw it together for yourself.

	Argument	Examples/evidence
Section 2		
Section 3		

	Argument	Examples/evidence
Section 4		
Section 5		

COMMENT _____

You should now have a good skeleton summary of the main argument of the chapter and the examples used to illustrate this. You can check this against the filled-in grid at the end of the workbook (pp.71–3) to see if you have misunderstood or missed out something vital. But remember, something in your own words is worth ten of anything supplied by the course team because it is the result of your own direct engagement with the course material.

The main thing to check is that you have successfully sorted the wood from the trees (i.e. the overall argument from the examples):

- Section 2 develops the argument about the relationship between scientific and common-sense knowledge, once again using the example of medicine from which to draw general points. It tells us lots of interesting things about the growth of medical science but this is only to illustrate the main argument about scientific knowledge. The section argues that scientific knowledge assumes that there is a separation between nature and culture, that the natural sciences are objective rather than subjective, and that it can therefore be used to investigate the world and discover the truth. It is also argued that it is organized in a way that excludes the common people and that the institutionalization and professionalization of knowledge was a prerequisite for the development of the idea of *objectivity* and the 'scientific method'.

- Sections 3 and 4 challenge this idea and develop the narrative of the social production of knowledge by looking at how natural science *actually* works and at the link between politics, science and society. In particular, the chapter looks at the influence of gender and the exclusion of women from certain spheres of knowledge and the devaluing of 'female' knowledge as compared to 'male'. The example of medicine is used to show how natural scientific knowledge is transmitted through institutions with authority and power over others and 'common-sense' knowledge is excluded.

- Section 5 concentrates on the relationships between knowledge and *practice* and how knowledge may be used for political ends.

1.2 Analytical strand: scientific and social scientific knowledge

As you can see from the summary above, one of the main themes in the narrative strand of this chapter is the development of the debate about the character of natural scientific and social scientific knowledge and methods. This in turn relates directly to the *analytical* aspect of knowledge and knowing. As we noted in the introduction to this workbook, different forms of knowledge depend on different kinds of evidence for support. The social sciences are a specialized form of knowledge and have their own way of gathering information and evidence and constructing explanations. Received wisdom would have it that the difference between science and social science lies in the methods which each uses to investigate phenomena and generate an understanding of how things work.

WORKBOOK ACTIVITY 1.3

Re-read Sections 2 and 3 of the chapter and list the words used to describe *scientific method*.

COMMENT

We had a quick glance and came up with a number of words which are said to characterize natural scientific method – for example, *theory, impartial, objective, controlled, experimental, repetition, double blind, scepticism, falsification, observation, reason, rigorous testing*. There are probably others that we missed.

Some scientists would say that the scientific method is quite different to the methods used by social scientists (and superior to them). But scientific knowledge depends on a process that looks very similar to the circuit of knowledge that we have used to describe social scientific methodology. Both begin by asking questions and developing claims, then look for evidence regarding those claims, then interpret the evidence and use this interpretation to act and change our understanding of the world. If we look at how science actually works the similarities seem even greater.

The main critique which philosophers and social scientists make of science is that it 'assumes that there is a measurable, material world, which can be investigated through scientific methods' (p.19). The chapter argues that Baconian scientific method is *not* objective, culture-free, inductive and rational and introduces a number of alternative views about the process of knowing which apply equally well to scientific and social scientific methods of investigation. These include those of academic commentators such as Foucault, Popper, Kuhn and Evelyn Fox Keller who, although they don't agree with one another, all emphasize in different ways the importance of different *discourses* (culture, language and social interaction) in arriving at versions of what may be perceived to be a truth.

Activity 1.4 on SIDS (Sudden Infant Death Syndrome) illustrates the authors' point that there are competing systems of knowledge which are heavily influenced by social factors, including, in this case, the distribution of power and authority and cultural assumptions about gender roles. The purpose of the case study is not to suggest that all cases of SIDS are concealed infanticide but to show how different explanations originate and how it comes about that some carry more weight than others. It highlights the fact that the 'true' answer to SIDS may never be found. Fresh evidence is constantly being brought forward, some of which contradicts previous beliefs, and it is most likely that multiple factors are involved rather than only one.

An important conclusion that this throws up is that we need to view the circuit of knowledge rather carefully. There is a temptation to see the circuit as a process separate from the rest of society whereby ideas and explanations are gradually improved and refined as we scientifically evaluate evidence and develop new hypotheses. In fact, it is not separate from society at all but implicated up to the hilt in the institutions and discourses of the day. To make this clear our representation of the circuit needs to be set in the context of its societal framework so that it looks like Figure 4.

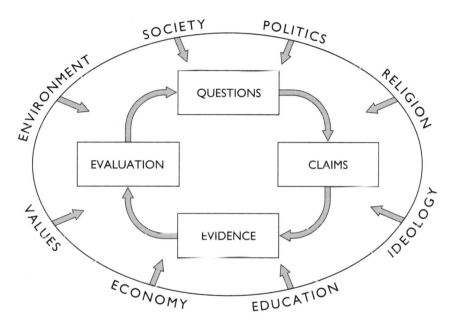

FIGURE 4   The circuit of knowledge in the context of its societal framework

1.3 Linking the course themes

Both the narrative and the analytical aspects of the *knowledge and knowing* theme are closely linked to the other two course themes, *structure and agency* and *uncertainty and diversity*. The structure and agency theme highlights the influence of social institutions and social processes on individuals' and groups' beliefs and actions. In the context of knowledge and knowing this leads us to ask how individual knowledge might be shaped and constrained by institutional factors and just what those factors might be. The uncertainty and diversity theme asks questions about the nature of social change and whether the UK has become a more diverse and uncertain and less stable society in the last 50 years or so. These, too, connect directly with both the knowledge and knowing narrative element, which looks at the changing nature of natural scientific and social scientific knowledge, and the analytical element, which emphasizes the extent to which all forms of knowledge are open to doubt. The medical example used in the chapter provides ample illustration of these points.

WORKBOOK ACTIVITY 1.4

Look back over your notes and previous grids, pick out specific examples that illustrate points relating to *structure and agency* and *uncertainty and diversity* and plot them on the grid below.

	Argument	Examples/evidence
Structure and agency		

	Argument	Examples/evidence
Uncertainty and diversity		

C O M M E N T

You should have been able to fill in your grid by simply reorganizing the notes that you made earlier, but you will need to take a few minutes to digest and think about the issues that are raised.

The example of medical knowledge shows us that there are a variety of different sources of knowledge. We can see that individual beliefs, interpretations and actions are constrained by social structures and cultural discourses. Nevertheless, there is still scope for variation and change in which individual agents can play a part. Uncertainty and diversity have always been a part of knowledge and knowing. Both natural science and social science have attempted to investigate and organize knowledge in a way that makes it manageable and testable but these methods can never be entirely objective. Expert knowledge is a means of legitimizing and restricting access to knowledge as a way of controlling it, but the interaction between social factors and other diverse forms of knowledge provides opportunities for change.

2 KNOWING AND BELIEVING: RELIGIOUS KNOWLEDGE

Chapter 1 argues that there are many different forms of knowledge, but it concentrates on scientific knowledge and remarks, almost in passing, that this has replaced religious belief as the dominant form in Western society. Chapter 2 explores this argument and takes as its main focus the question of the nature and status of religious belief, how this relates to other forms of knowledge and how it interacts with other social factors. By now you will not be surprised to find that answering this question isn't exactly straightforward and entails asking many more questions before the authors can even approach a conclusion!

KEY TASKS

Chapter 2, 'Knowing and Believing: Religious Knowledge'.

- To distinguish between *substantive* and *functional* definitions of religion.

- To be able to compare *positivist* and *interpretative* methods of investigating religion.

- To use evidence about gender, ethnicity and New Age beliefs to evaluate the theories which are put forward.

Now please read Chapter 2, 'Knowing and Believing: Religious Knowledge' and then return to this point in the workbook.

2.1 Narrative strand: the status of religious knowledge

In the first place the chapter deals with the question of the status of religious belief as a form of knowledge. Then it looks at the practice of religion in the contemporary UK, whether this is in decline or not and how it is influenced by social factors such as gender and ethnicity. Finally it examines diverse forms of belief and the ways in which these relate to conventional religion and to other forms of social change.

2.1.1 Identifying the argument

You can identify the main points in the narrative argument of the chapter by looking at the summaries for Section 2.1 (on the nature of religion), Section 3 (secularization), Section 4 (gender and religion), Section 5 (ethnicity), and Section 6 (New Age beliefs and extrasensory experiences).

The first question which is asked is about the status of religious belief as a form of knowledge and how it differs from natural scientific knowledge.

WORKBOOK ACTIVITY 2.1

Activity 2.2 in Chapter 2 (p.48) asks you to identify *differences* between religion and science. That there is such a difference is clearly illustrated by the extract below.

When you have read the extract:

- Ask yourself why the author of the article does not believe that creationist beliefs are a legitimate form of knowledge.

- Make brief notes on the reasons he gives for his conclusion.

Where Darwin is a dirty word

Keith Devlin

Any British academic who drains their brain across the Atlantic soon finds there is a lot of truth in the quip that Britain and America are 'two countries divided by a common language'. For a British university scientist who makes the big trip, one startling discovery is that a staggering 44% of Americans believe the biblical story of creation is absolutely true. For almost half the US population, both the Big Bang theory and the theory of evolution by natural selection are rejected outright. And this in a country that leads the world in scientific discoveries and technological advances, whose universities and research laboratories are homes to more Nobel prizewinners than anywhere else, and whose vast resources put a man on the Moon.

Fresh off the plane, you are likely to meet some of that 44% the moment you step into a classroom. How do you teach science to someone who refuses to entertain the overwhelming mass of evidence that makes the principles of evolution by natural selection one of the most sure pieces of scientific knowledge we have? It doesn't help to point out that the evidence for evolution is more certain than much of the medical knowledge these students rely on when they fall sick.

I first met this attitude in 1990. Three years earlier, I had left Lancaster University for a two-year research position at Stanford University, and then moved on to a prestigious private college in the US.

As a mathematician, I don't normally teach evolution, but I had to lead a general education course for non-science students in one class. (In the US, many institutions insist all students take some maths and science classes.) I began by showing the class the first part of Stanley Kubrick's classic movie, *2001: A Space Odyssey*, which shows our ape-like ancestors discovering language, learning, knowledge and tool use, and ends with a bone tossed into the air turning into a modern space ship.

I aimed to use the movie to help explain how maths and science are conceptual tools we use in addition to our physical tools. But the class took an unexpected turn when one young man took exception to the film, and to my assumption that Darwin's standard story of human evolution was pretty well accepted. What had been planned as a course on the nature and uses of maths became, of necessity, an attempt on my part to explain the nature of science and how it is done. But it was an uphill battle I never won.

My main antagonist was bright and articulate and – apart from his huge ignorance about the scientific method – extremely well educated and widely read. Frankly, I found it quite scary to encounter such blindness towards evidence in someone with such ability.

I am not talking about belief in God here. But while no scientific evidence suggests there is no God, there is a mountain of evidence that is incompatible with a literal interpretation of the Genesis story of the creation, which implies that the entire world was created in more or less its present form – complete with Adam and Eve – about 10,000 years ago.

The issue of teaching evolution in schools hit the US headlines recently, when the Kansas Board of Education voted to remove all mention of evolution from the state's school science curriculum. In doing so, it joined Alabama, New Mexico and Nebraska, which have also placed severe restrictions on the teaching of evolution in schools.

Over a decade ago, the US Supreme Court decreed that states could not compel the teaching of creationism. Since then, the creationists – a large and powerful, right-wing lobby group – have been trying to push Darwin out, or at least make sure it is presented as 'just one opinion'.

In Alabama, any school textbook that discusses evolution must carry a warning that says 'This textbook discusses evolution, a controversial theory some scientists present as a scientific explanation for the origin of living things, such as plants, animals and humans. No one was present when life first appeared on earth. Therefore, any statement about life's origins should be considered as theory, not fact.'

Because state legislatures cannot exert the same control over universities, lecturers have much greater freedom in what and how we teach it. But we have to teach the students the schools produce. Even at my college, in the highly pro-science state of California, I regularly meet students who think science is 'just one person's opinion'.

This, I think, is where the real problem lies for the educator. How can you teach science to someone who has reached 18 and thinks it's about which ideas you find the most appealing? Having that student in your class four hours a week for one or two semesters is unlikely to overcome the effects of 12 years of school education. University education can build on school; it's hard to overturn what was learned in school. To get the basic ideas of science across, you have to accept the framework in which science operates.

The US academic waters are indeed inviting. But for some students you will meet, you will have to explain what science is and try to convince them that the entire enterprise has merit. Nothing you will have experienced in the UK will have prepared you for that.

Source: *Guardian Higher*, 14 September 1999

COMMENT

The author rejects creationism not because it is a religious belief but because its adherents will not accept the need for 'scientific' verification – the use of experimental methods and proofs to validate theories and hypotheses. To him this cannot be knowledge and can only be classified as ignorance or superstition.

The extract emphasizes the differences between evolutionary theory and creationist beliefs but it struck us that although there is undoubtedly a difference between the rational nature of science and the spiritual nature of religion there are aspects of the acceptance of both as knowledge which are surprisingly similar (compare the discussion on Audio-cassette 9, Side A). Both are legitimized by a form of authority, both are produced through particular language, both are institutionalized, and there are symbols and rituals in science that can acquire an almost religious significance to some adherents! That these aspects tend to be the *social aspects* of the two different forms of knowledge reinforces the argument of Chapter 1 that 'knowledge' is neither absolute nor divorced from its context but is socially constructed and conditioned.

This point is developed in the discussion of the definition of religion in Section 2. Most people think of religion as involving a belief in God, the existence of some kind of spiritual element in the world over and above what can be discovered by the natural sciences and some kind of moral code that we should live by. Social scientists have been more analytical and Section 2 identifies two main types of definition – substantive and functional.

WORKBOOK ACTIVITY 2.2

To make sure that you understand this distinction re-read Section 2 and then make a note of the two definitions below, using your own words and giving an example of each.

	Definition	Example
Substantive		
Functional		

C O M M E N T _____

According to Section 2 the substantive definition of religion concerns its content (e.g. beliefs, practices and hierarchies) and the functional definition focuses on its purpose. But how helpful is this? The distinction between the two is exemplified in the work of two of the key thinkers in the social sciences, Max Weber and Emile Durkheim. Each saw religion as having an important influence in different ways but at the same time each included both substantive and functional aspects in their approach.

Weber's approach to religion is said to be largely 'substantive', in that he concentrated on the specific beliefs and practices of Protestantism, but there are also functional aspects. He was interested in Protestant beliefs not for their own sake but, as Chapter 2 says (pp.48–9), because of 'their ethical implications for individuals' economic behaviour, and the role played by this economic behaviour in the development of seventeenth-century capitalism'. In other words, because of the function they performed in a specific society.

Durkheim's definition also included both substantive and functional aspects. He defined religion substantively – the 'sacred' as opposed to the 'profane' – but the main thrust of his argument was functionalist in that it saw religion as serving a social purpose by uniting individuals in a shared community. The logical conclusion of this argument is that almost anything can be a religion, provided it combines the necessary features of 'a unified system of beliefs and practices relative to sacred things, that is to say, things set apart and forbidden' (Durkheim, 1912/1965, p.21).

WORKBOOK ACTIVITY 2.3

Section 2.1 lists some examples of belief systems that perform the same social functions as religion. Can you think of others? Remember the definition above and make a note of the 'sacred' element of the belief as well as rituals, symbols and ceremonies that may bind people together.

C O M M E N T _____

We hope you have managed to think of at least one example of your own. If you do that instead of using the ones given to you, you not only get to practice applying the ideas but you will probably remember them more easily too. The one we thought of was football. The local team is sacred to its supporters; they are united into a close community by their belief; the trainer or manager plays the role of high priest; certain objects and places such as the football ground, the team scarf and strip have symbolic significance; and there are rituals and chants known only to the initiates. This may seem a rather trivial example but for local communities and, indeed, for whole nations, football teams create a sense of belonging and identity and in that sense do serve the kind of integrative social function which Durkheim says is performed by religion.

The definition of religion that is used is important because it will influence any conclusions that are drawn about the 'secularization' of society and the status that religion is given in comparison with competing systems such as natural science. The substantive perspective defines religion in terms of the content of specific beliefs and practices embodying a particular form of knowledge. In contrast, the functionalist perspective sees religion *not* as a form of knowledge but as a social institution, not much different from the family or the education system, with a social role to perform.

In terms of the secularization debate, functionalists and 'substantivists' take a different position. Those who take a functionalist perspective would argue that as long as religion performs a function in society it will persist in some form. Those who take a substantive approach would argue that because there has been a decline in conventional religious practice this means that the status of religion as a recognized form of knowledge is in decline.

2.2 Using the course themes

2.2.1 Belief, uncertainty and diversity

Before the rise of modern science it was through organized religion that people knew and explained phenomena and tried to work out their place in the order of things. This is still the case in some parts of the Christian world and in most parts of the Islamic world. Elsewhere, it has been argued, scientific rationalism has undermined and replaced religious belief as our main way of understanding the world. But is this really true or is it the case, as others have argued, that the failures of science have driven more people to search for spiritual answers to questions about the meaning of life?

As Western society has become more educated, more democratic, and more individualized power has become more distributed. The authority of structures such as the hierarchies of the established churches has been diminished and challenged from both inside and outside. Feminists have attacked the patriarchal nature of the main religions and there has been increasing exposure to different cultures and access to alternative forms of belief. In religion, as in science, there is undoubtedly now more diversity. Religious knowledge and belief have a different meaning in different social and cultural settings and religion may serve different purposes for different groups. In other words, like other forms of knowledge, belief is not static but adaptable according to social factors such as changes in gender roles and increased ethnic diversity.

2.2.2 Structure and agency

Different approaches to religion put a different emphasis on the relative importance of structure and agency. Both the substantive and the functionalist definitions see religion as performing a structural role in society, but the substantive definition places a particular emphasis on the importance of the institutions and hierarchies of organized forms of religion while the functionalist definition would include other kinds of belief systems, such as nationalism or the women's movement, which perform the same social function as traditional religions.

Berger, on the other hand, highlights the importance of individual agency. He sees religion as performing a personal rather than a social function by providing a system of meaning which allows us to make sense of the great mystery of life and death. What is important is not the established structure of the church (or other belief systems) or the role that they play in society but the individual's sense of spirituality and personal identity.

This aspect is present to some extent in most religions and it is particularly stressed in those which have rejected all forms of priestly hierarchy (the Quakers for example). It is also present in forms of New Age belief, many of which emphasize the inner life of the individual and ideas of harmony with nature rather than traditional forms of religious organization and observance.

WORKBOOK ACTIVITY 2.4

What evidence is given in the chapter to support the view that:

- Changing gender roles have affected religion?

- Increased ethnic diversity has influenced religious knowledge and meaning in the UK?

- There was an increase in New Age beliefs in the latter part of the twentieth century in the UK?

How convincing do you find that evidence?

COMMENT _____

These questions aren't as straightforward as they look! There is certainly lots of evidence produced about these issues but first of all you need to keep at the back of your mind the *prior* question of the definition of religion. In this respect you should note that although the evidence on the role of gender covers both Western and Eastern traditional forms of religion and New Age beliefs, the latter is not explicitly covered in the section on ethnicity. Does this matter? Maybe not, but it would have been interesting to see whether there is any connection between increased ethnic diversity and the stated growth in New Age beliefs. We might ask ourselves why it wasn't included. It could be that there is no evidence on this or that the authors simply chose not to include it.

Gender. Evidence is presented to show that although in the past women were poorly represented in the hierarchies of most religions, their increasing involvement in other public spheres has meant that male dominance in the church has also been challenged. The admission of women to the priesthood of the Church of England has consequently led to changes in practice and in belief. In particular the doctrine that patriarchy is religiously sanctioned by God has been rejected by many believers, leading those who continue to subscribe to this view to transfer their allegiance to other churches or bishops. Some women have extended the arena of belief and spirituality beyond the bounds of conventional religion to form broader alternative movements with a spiritual dimension such as eco-feminism.

Ethnicity. As Table 2.4 illustrates, UK society is increasingly diverse and there are a large number of different religious communities. Different religions may offer different explanations and world-views and they may perform specific social functions for minority ethnic groups. For example, religious identity may reinforce social solidarity within separate communities or it may provide an alternative value system to that of the majority community.

New Age beliefs. There are many different kinds of New Age belief so once again we need to be careful about what we are talking about. This lack of precision makes collecting evidence more difficult. The chapter talks about New Age beliefs both in terms of the sacred spreading over into the secular sphere, as for example in some forms of ecologism, and in terms of the

" D'you think there's anything in this astrology business?"

appropriation of natural scientific ideas into some alternative belief systems. The definition used covers a wide variety of such beliefs. Maybe too wide to be meaningful?

The evidence offered for the view that there was an increase in New Age beliefs at the end of the twentieth century includes the growth in the number of books on the occult and surveys and interviews conducted by the Religious Experience Research Unit at the University of Oxford and the Religious Experience Research Project at Nottingham University. How we evaluate this information and what conclusions we reach about the nature of religion as a form of knowledge and the way in which it interacts with society depends to a large extent on the methodology which is used to analyse the data. This is dealt with in Section 2.1 of the chapter and is discussed below.

2.3 Analytical strand: investigating religion

On the one hand, it is claimed that social change and advances in natural scientific knowledge have run counter to religious beliefs and have led to increased secularization. On the other hand, there seems to have been a growth in interest in alternative beliefs which can be seen as a response to the undermining of conventional forms of religion and scientific knowledge by the increasing diversity and uncertainty of modern society. We can all give our own opinion about the question but in order to assess the various claims which are made we need to investigate the evidence for the arguments which are put forward.

Chapter 2 distinguishes between *positivist* and *interpretative* approaches to the investigation of religion (Section 2.2.1). They sound complicated but don't be alarmed. These are just social science names for something that is quite easy to grasp. To help you we have constructed a grid summarizing the main features of each.

WORKBOOK ACTIVITY 2.5

Check through the grid below and then fill in the strengths and weaknesses of the two methods and an example of each taken from the chapter.

	Positivist	Interpretative
Assumptions	We can only learn about the world and about people and social relations through observation of what people do.	Acknowledges the agency and understanding of human subjects. Takes account of the intentions of both subjects and researchers.
Methods	Observation and measurement. Uses quantitative methods, e.g. collection and analysis of statistical data. Seeks to make causal links, to construct general laws and establish structural explanations.	Uses qualitative methods which allow for a variety of perspectives and meanings, e.g. interview.
Strengths		
Weaknesses		

	Positivist	Interpretative
Example		

C O M M E N T

The kind of method chosen to investigate religion depends very much on the definition of religion which is used by the researcher. Those who think that religion is a matter of institutions, hierarchies and formalized practices are happy to rely on positivist methods which can measure such things. On the other hand, for those who believe that religion is defined not by the function it performs in society or by formal content but by the meaning which it has for the individual and its ability to provide some kind of explanation of the purpose of life, what people *think* and *feel* is of vital importance. For these researchers the interpretative approach is the one which will provide the answers. Each method has strengths and weaknesses.

The *strength* of the positivist approach is that it provides concrete data that can be used to support or rebut the claims made by social scientists. For example, the amount of adult church attendance, the number of people who believe in God, the difference in belief between men and women, and the size of the total religious community in the UK. Its *weakness* is that it treats human behaviour without reference to the human concerns of the subject which may give the action a completely different meaning to that understood by the researcher. For example, an individual's failure to attend church might be because of a lack of religious belief but it might be because the individual disagrees with the emphasis of that church (e.g. too male, too 'high' or too 'low') or because she subscribes to a different kind of belief (e.g. some form of New Age belief). At the same time we need to remember that even when positivist methods are used results will be influenced by the interpretation of the researcher. Positivist research is *not* free of human bias and can be influenced by values and beliefs as much as can interpretative research.

The *strength* of the interpretative approach is that it supplies this missing *qualitative* element, i.e. it allows more scope for individuals to put their own interpretation on questions and to give a more personal and diverse response (on the utility of qualitative evidence see *Study Skills Supplement 2: Reading*

Evidence, Section 3). The examples given by the authors are the use of interviews which allow women to express their own views and experiences about religion and in-depth interviews exploring individuals' religious experiences. Other examples (not expanded on in the chapter) are the use of fiction, art and music as a source of evidence and the use of *participant observation* which allows an investigator to participate in and include her or his own experiences of the subject under investigation as a legitimate piece of evidence.

The *weakness* of the interpretative approach is that because it operates in the realm of feelings and opinion the evidence is not subject to the same level of verification as quantitative evidence. It is hard to come up with a reliable way of finding out what people really feel about spiritual matters. Even if we could ask everybody how would we know that their accounts were reliable? They might not be prepared to say anything at all, they might lie and say what they thought we wanted to hear or they might not even know how they felt themselves. This is illustrated by the examination of New Age beliefs and extrasensory experiences with which the chapter concludes. When faced with the question of whether or not there has been an increase in belief in religious knowledge the authors find that statistical evidence is scarce and that it is difficult to define terms and to draw conclusions when faced with the different kinds of interpretative evidence which are available.

Other workbooks have already drummed into you one of the fundamental rules of social science. *Evidence does not speak for itself.* It is one thing to collect evidence about religious belief, or anything else for that matter, but then we have to interpret what it means. This is particularly true of qualitative data but it also applies to quantitative data. Because of the authority accorded to the scientific method statistics may be seen as being more accurate and reliable – so much so that social scientists often present the results of interpretative studies in a quantitative form. As we have pointed out, however, positivist studies are also influenced by definitions, assumptions, blind spots and other external factors.

Researchers have tried to overcome these problems by combining different kinds of approach; for example, using positivist tools such as surveys and experiments to test subjective accounts of spiritual experiences. However, there is almost always more than one interpretation that can be put on the evidence. The evidence on falling church attendance can be interpreted as 'proving' the secularization thesis. On the other hand, the figures on religious belief suggest that far more people hold religious beliefs than go to church and what people have to say about their own experiences adds yet another dimension. It is for this reason that social scientists tend to prefer to use more than one method and to use evidence not as a means of finally answering a question but as a way of generating new questions.

3 POLITICAL IDEOLOGIES AND THE ENVIRONMENT

Chapters 1 and 2 have illustrated how different forms of knowledge are produced and how natural science and social science use different kinds of methodology to investigate the world. As we noted in the introduction to this workbook, social science knowledge is organized around *theories* about the nature of the social world and *ideologies* which are a set of beliefs and values about how things ought to be and how change can be brought about. There are a variety of different ideologies. For example, Block 3 identified *conservatism*, *social democracy*, *liberalism*, *Marxism* and *feminism* as political ideologies that have influenced the way that we think about social issues and problems, Chapter 2 of this block has shown how religious ideology provides an alternative world-view, and there are, of course, plenty of other ideologies which are not dealt with in this course.

In the same way that theories are tested through the process of the *circuit of knowledge* ideologies are also tested and developed. We choose between different ideologies partly on the basis of how closely they fit with our own vision of the kind of society that we want to see but also on the basis of their accuracy and usefulness in analysing social situations and prescribing ways of dealing with the social world. If the old ideologies are found wanting in this respect it is necessary to develop new ideas that provide better explanations and policies. This is the process that is examined in Chapter 3 in respect of the development of the new ideology of *ecologism* as a response to other ideologies' failure adequately to explain and suggest remedies for the problems of the global environment.

KEY TASKS

Chapter 3, 'Political Ideologies and the Environment'.

- To revisit the concept of political *ideology*.

- To clarify the role of different ideologies in respect of environmental policy.

- To apply the course themes to the comparison between different ideologies.

- To identify the main features of *ecologism*.

- To use the *circuit of knowledge* to evaluate different theories about the environment.

 Now please read Chapter 3, 'Political Ideologies and the Environment' and then return to this point in the workbook.

3.1 Narrative strand: knowledge, ideology and the environment

In the same way that Chapter 1 might seem to be 'about' medicine there is a chance that you might fall into the trap of thinking that this chapter is about the environment. So let's dispel that idea straight away and look for the underlying argument relating to knowledge.

3.1.1 Identifying the argument

If you go back to Section 1, you will see that the main theme of the chapter is not the environment as such, but the way that environmental change has challenged our way of thinking and the knowledge that we thought we had about the world. We are not just talking about abstract theories here but about the political ideologies which are responsible for determining how we respond to problems and approach their solution. This is important, not just because it shows us how knowledge evolves, but also because it shows how forms of knowledge and ideology have a direct bearing on practical issues such as the survival of the planet.

If you check Section 1 you will see that it identifies four questions which provide a framework for this chapter. The chapter is concerned with the interaction between political ideology and the environment. It asks:

- What is political ideology and why is it important?

- What are the practical challenges to conventional political ideology posed by environmental degradation?

- How have conventional political ideologies responded to these problems?

- What is the nature of green thinking and how does it differ from conventional political ideologies?

Political ideologies

It is argued that political ideologies are important because they are different ways of understanding (or knowing) the social world and they provide us with a choice of alternative courses of action which will affect the way that society develops and changes. The chapter deals with the three 'mainstream' political ideologies to which you were introduced in Block 3 (and to a lesser extent their Marxist and feminist critiques) and considers their approach to environmental problems. Before we tackle this it would be useful to recap on the main features of each of these in respect of four different aspects – their approach to human nature, politics, economy and social change.

You will find it useful to refer back to your notes on Block 3 here. You may also find your notes on Book 2, Chapter 3 on the market and environmental problems useful.

The grid below shows first the three 'mainstream' ideologies – conservatism, liberalism and social democracy – and then the two main critiques of these, Marxism and feminism.

	Human nature	Politics	Economy	Social change
Conservatism	Imperfect, static; inequalities innate and inevitable.	Emphasis on stability, hierarchy, elite leadership, traditional institutions and 'nationhood'.	Emphasis on rural economy, small firms, traditional industries, low level of state intervention.	Continuity is more important than change. When inevitable, change should be managed by strong leadership.
Liberalism	Self interested.	Emphasis on individual rights and freedoms, minimum state intervention.	Emphasis on competitive markets as the best way of allocating resources and ensuring economic growth; minimum state intervention.	Markets ought to be liberalized so as to allow the 'invisible hand' of the market to bring about equilibrium without state intervention.
Social democracy	A function of social circumstances; improvable by changing conditions.	Emphasis on keeping a balance between interest groups with a democratic state acting as a neutral 'referee' and providing minimum standards.	Emphasis on management of a mixed economy with the state regulating private enterprise and providing welfare and essential services when necessary.	Change ought to be gradual and managed by the democratic state.
Marxism	People can change their nature depending on social circumstances and their own activity.	All societies are divided into classes according to the dominant system of economic production. The dominant class uses the organization of the state to control society in its own interests. Class conflict and changes in the system of production lead to new political systems.	Ownership and control over the means of production determines who benefits from society; the economy should be democratically controlled by the workers, either directly or through the state, and wealth distributed according to need.	Change occurs through class struggle. Full equality can only be brought about by the revolutionary overthrow of the ruling class.
Feminism	Human nature is innately ungendered but is conditioned by gender relations in society.	The personal is political. Society is patriarchal, women are excluded from power, social roles are organized to support this; gender inequalities are institutionalized.	The economy is supported by low female wages and the unpaid reproductive labour of women. Women should earn equal pay and be recompensed for their domestic labour or share this with men.	Real social change is not possible without a fundamental change in gender relations.

You will see that each ideology has distinctive features with different implications for policy decisions in a variety of social spheres. These have come about through a process of reaction to and modification of previous ideologies and their application.

Environmental challenges

Although the mainstream political ideologies differ from each other in many ways, it is argued that they share a common tendency which poses particular problems when dealing with environmental problems:

- a belief in a notion of progress which is centred on economic growth

- an approach based on the organization of politics on a national basis

- the placing of human beings in a privileged position at the centre of the universe.

WORKBOOK ACTIVITY 3.1

Re-read Section 2 and make a list of the reasons given for saying that environmental problems pose a challenge to these particular approaches.

COMMENT

Ideas about progress which are incorporated in the mainstream ideologies hinge on the belief that this can be brought about by applying the natural sciences and technology to eliminate both natural problems, such as drought, and social ills, such as poverty or famine, thus improving the lot of everybody. But environmental problems are not the result of a simple process of cause and effect involving single factors. They tend to be multi-factoral – that is, they are the product of a complex series of interrelationships which cannot be controlled or predicted. For this reason, attempts to bring about some desired improvement or to solve a particular environmental problem by the application of science are unlikely to succeed and may well have the opposite effect to what is intended.

The problem is made worse by the organization of this idea of progress and development through nation-states which act in their own political and economic interests. In the course of trying to improve the lot of their own citizens nations have inevitably taken a partial view of both the costs and the benefits of any particular action and ignored the total environmental consequences. At the same time it has proved impossible for individual states to overcome environmental problems which are worldwide in their nature.

Finally, it is argued that treating human beings as if they are not part of nature but somehow above it, with superior ethical rights, leads to a fatal blindness about the limits to human capacities. Behaving as if we are lords of all we survey, manipulating nature and even interfering with the genetic structure of life itself might lead to irreversible damage which we are powerless to repair.

Conventional responses

The kinds of solution to these environmental problems which are offered by mainstream political ideologies are divided into two separate camps according to their analysis of the problem and the solution offered. We have mapped these on the grid below.

	Liberalism	Conservatism and social democracy
Analysis	Environmental problems are caused because market mechanisms do not operate.	Environmental problems arise because market mechanisms are not appropriate for environmental management (conservatism). Environmental resources cannot and should not be individually owned, therefore a collective solution must be found (social democracy).
Solution	Establish ownership rights and prices and then allow the market to operate. If this is not possible use the agency of the state.	Non intervention in the natural environment (conservatism). Democratic decision making. Intervene using the agency of the state (social democracy).

Green thinking

The radical ecologists' critique of both of these approaches hinges on their rejection of instrumentalism and anthropocentrism and their adoption of a different worldview and a completely different set of values. In order to assess this critique we must therefore explore those two concepts and get to grips with exactly what they mean and what the implications of the radical stance would be.

WORKBOOK ACTIVITY 3.2

Think about the argument and then jot down your own definitions of the two terms below. Remember, what we are interested in is not just a dictionary definition but a considered explanation of the concepts as they are used here.

Instrumentality

Anthropocentrism

COMMENT

It is clear that when environmentalists refer to instrumentalism and anthropocentrism they are not just using the terms descriptively. Green thinking incorporates a specific view of the ethical relationship between human beings and nature which translates into a political view on the kinds of policy which should be adopted. Instrumentality – the idea of using nature to serve human ends – is frowned on, not because it won't work (that would just be continuing to take an instrumental approach) but because it is seen as ethically wrong. The same is true of anthropocentrism – the belief that the interests of the human species are paramount above all others. Environmentalists oppose policies based on this approach because they put the interests of nature itself above those of just one species.

"THEY USED TO BE THOUGHT OF AS CRACKPOTS."

'Green' alternatives have developed as a critique of existing political ideologies. They argue that conventional theories and explanations are inadequate when it comes to finding solutions to environmental problems and purport to offer an alternative perspective which organizes knowledge in a different way.

WORKBOOK ACTIVITY 3.3

1   What is the difference between *ecology* and *ecologism*?

2   What are the key features of the ecological perspective and how does it differ from the approach of the dominant political ideologies of the twentieth century?

Remember to use <u>your own words</u> or use quotation marks with a page reference.

C O M M E N T

1 The history of the evolution of ecologism shows clearly the incorporation of different kinds of knowledge – including the science of 'relations between organisms and their environment', the study of animal and human behaviour, Greek moral philosophy, and the second law of thermo-dynamics – into the ideology of ecologism that involves a theory about how the world works, social values about how things *ought* to be, and a political programme of action. It is particularly interesting to see how ecologism takes concepts such as energy and efficiency, which are used by physicists and economists, and applies them in a different context.

2 The key features of ecologism and the main differences between this and mainstream political ideologies are mapped on the table which the chapter develops for Activities 3.1–3.5 and 3.7 which is reproduced here as Table 1.

TABLE 1   Summary of environmental problems for political ideologies (Table 3.2 from Chapter 3)

	Environmental problems of modern political ideologies	Responses of modern political ideologies	The challenge of green thinking	Green alternatives
Economics	Continued world-wide industrialization is not environmentally sustainable.	The problem is not one of how *much* growth but what *kind* of growth to pursue.	Environmental problems are often unknown and complex.	Reorganize society away from material growth towards spiritual development.
	The market cannot solve environmental problems.	Many environmental problems can be solved by markets if environmental resources are owned and priced properly.	Money is not the measure of everything. What about the future?	Replace the market with self-sufficiency and direct popular control.
Politics	Environmental problems are typically global in their causes and effects, whereas political authority and control is exercised on a national basis.	International co-operation is possible on the basis of self-interest among states, especially when knowledge about the problem is available and agreed.	If problems are global in scope, then we must move beyond the nation-state and organize politics at a global level as well.	Encourage the development of global citizenship and reconstitute political authority at a global level through extending the UN system.
Culture	Environmental problems are evidence that we cannot subject nature to our control without creating problems.	We are part of nature and therefore we must take an enlightened view of our own interests, which include a healthy environment.	Enlightened self-interest is still *self*-interest (it's human-centred), but what about the interests of the rest of nature?	Respect and protect the interests of the non-human natural world. Need for a new spiritualism. Need for non-reductionist, non-individualistic forms of thinking.

The main claim of green alternatives is that they place nature, not humanity, at the centre of the equation. We need to be careful, however, not to over-simplify by boiling things down too much. It is important to define terms before accepting claims by one side or the other. Since the idea of 'nature' is central to the argument we need to recognize that the term is used in different ways. It is not just descriptive. It is not value free and we need to assess the arguments put forward by ecologists as rigorously as we do those which are put forward by other political ideologists.

3.2 Using the course themes

As we noted above, it can be argued that mainstream ideologies are inadequate to explain and produce solutions for environmental problems for three reasons:

1   They are bounded by the nation-state.

2   They depend on the idea of scientific certainty.

3   They treat nature and society as separate entities.

The way that we think about these claims can be organized around the three course themes.

3.2.1 Structure and agency

A major obstacle to the solution of environmental problems is one of structure and agency. It is clear that environmental problems are not national in scope, but political power is. The structure of world power depends on the existence of nation-states and, although there are a number of international agencies, it is the sovereign state which is the locus of decision making and the principal agent when it comes to both the initiation of many environmental problems and the implementation of policies to overcome these problems.

Critics of mainstream ideologies argue that their analysis of society fails to take account of the mismatch between the global structure of the problem and the role of national agencies. In assessing this evidence Simon Bromley looks at both sides of the question. Does the fact that mainstream ideologies do not envisage the end of the nation-state mean that they cannot provide any solutions to environmental problems? There are certainly difficulties imposed by international structures but, on the other hand, attaining the only alternative proposed – some supra-national form of power – could be even more difficult than achieving agreement through co-operation or bargaining between sovereign states. Should we work with what we've got or put our energies into changing structures?

'Next one, please!' – *'Progress' versus internationalism*

3.2.2 Knowledge and knowing

Green alternatives don't only question the structures for dealing with environmental problems. They also question our way of knowing about them. As we pointed out in Chapters 1 and 2, there are a variety of different forms of knowledge. Simon Bromley examines two criticisms of the role of scientific knowledge in understanding and prescribing solutions for environmental problems. First, he assesses the claim by Giddens and Beck that the Western prioritization of scientific knowledge over other forms of knowledge and belief is reflected in the ideologies of modernity with their ideas about 'taming' and controlling nature. Second, he looks at the claim of many ecologists that the natural scientific approach is not something neutral but something which reflects and supports existing (particularly male) systems of authority.

WORKBOOK ACTIVITY 3.4

Look back over Chapters 1 and 2 for any evidence which you might be able to use in discussing these arguments.

COMMENT _____

There are a number of examples that you could use. For example, if you turn to Chapter 1 you will find that the discussion of the medical profession provides evidence about the way in which knowledge is socially produced and controlled by the structures of authority. The discussion of the functional role of religion in Chapter 2 highlights the interconnection between knowledge and society and previous chapters in the course also alert you to the role of values even when we are talking about knowledge and science.

_____

What environmentalists are doing when they reject abstract science for spiritual beliefs and more holistic theories is looking for other forms of understanding to support their own social values and world view. If we look at the *evidence* it seems that some of the blanket claims made by environmentalists about the mainstream ideologists' attitude to natural science and technology are not borne out. For example, although 'scientific Marxism' is based on the belief that we can understand and control the environment conservative ideology is extremely sceptical about this and about the idea of 'progress' generally. At the same time not all ecologists reject science as a means of understanding and finding solutions to environmental problems.

3.2.3 Uncertainty and diversity

The course has already introduced you to the idea that society is not simple. Although social scientists attempt to explain, predict and prescribe we are, and always will be, uncertain about many aspects. We live with risk in all aspects of our lives. If we make a personal mistake we must live with the consequences. If a doctor gets things wrong her patients may die. In the context of the nation-state, policies based on faulty social science or political ideology may lead to disaster for millions of people. The same risk applies when natural scientists and social scientists are dealing with environmental problems, only this time it is the future of the planet itself which is at stake.

The kind of interrelationships which exist between different parts of the environment mean that we can never be certain of the results of human intervention. Human beings have always interacted with and modified the environment. The question which the chapter addresses is whether recent advances in science have made this process qualitatively different to what has gone before and whether or not it requires a new kind of theory to understand and analyse it.

WORKBOOK ACTIVITY 3.5

Consider the discussion in Chapter 3, Sections 3 and 4 and identify the different arguments and evidence which would be used by mainstream ideologists and environmentalists in answering the following questions:

- Is science now the enemy of progress or the saviour of society?

- Is society at greater risk than ever before?

- Is it possible to find local solutions to environmental problems?

COMMENT

There are no right answers to these questions! To radical ecologists they aren't even the right questions, because they separate the idea of society from the rest of the environment. Nevertheless, how we analyse the problem – whether or not we adopt the mainstream view of our ability to control the environment or the ecological view of the environment as an integrated system   will have a significant effect on the policies which are adopted and on the final outcome. As Section 5 of Chapter 3 points out, the debate between different ideologies can be seen within the framework of the *circuit of knowledge*. The approach of different ideologies is put to the test, modified and tested again, with new answers and new questions constantly evolving.

3.3 Analytical strand: ideology and the circuit of knowledge

Chapter 3 uses the framework of the *circuit of knowledge* to test and evaluate the claims of the rival ideologies (Figure 5).

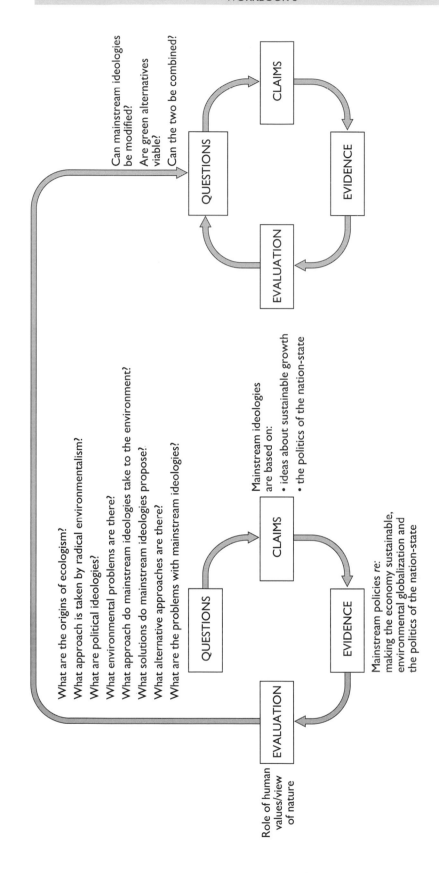

FIGURE 5 Chapter 3 mapped on to the circuit of knowledge

Divided into four steps we can trace the circuit as follows:

- Step 1 defines terms, explores the origins of the ecological perspective and identifies the major features of the argument.

- Step 2 compares the response to environmental problems by mainstream ideologies and radical ecologism.

- Step 3 examines the evidence in relation to specific aspects of the argument (the role of the nation-state and the effect of modern science).

- Step 4 outlines the way in which established ideologies have been modified and an alternative green ideology has been developed.

It is important to note that, as in Chapter 2, there is a mixture of evidence. Some of it is quantitative and refers to measurable aspects of environmental problems, for example. But much of it is qualitative and is directly affected by ideas about ethics and values. In the realms of political ideology these are as important as so-called facts and everything is open to contention – both between the traditional mainstream ideologies and between these and new ideologies such as ecologism.

Environmental change has led to changes in ideology and changes in ideology in turn have an impact on the kind of change which takes place in society. It is this process which is explored in Chapter 4.

4 LIVING IN THE AFTER-LIFE: KNOWLEDGE AND SOCIAL CHANGE

As we noted at the beginning of the workbook, this block contains both an analytical strand and a narrative strand relating to *knowledge and knowing*. The analytical strand uses the circuit of knowledge to examine the process by which we come to say that we 'know' something. The narrative strand explores the nature of 'knowledge' itself and how it is not constant but forever changing. In Chapter 1 you saw how the natural sciences, medicine and the social sciences have developed and produced different forms of knowledge; in Chapter 2 you looked at the nature of religious belief; and in Chapter 3 at new challenges to conventional wisdom about the environment.

Chapter 4 deals with one of the key questions for this block – the role of knowledge in both bringing about and understanding social change. It does so by examining three current theories about the kind of social change that has been taking place over the last decade or so. These are not the *only* theories which have been put forward and none of them (so far at least) has attained the status of the 'meta' (all-embracing) theories of the giants of social science theory such as Marx and Weber. Nevertheless, they do directly address those issues which are pivotal to our concerns in this block.

KEY TASKS

Chapter 4, 'Living in the After-life: Knowledge and Social Change'.

- To understand and be able to summarize the features of three theories about social change: the knowledge society, the fragmented society, and the risk society.

- To relate these theories to the three course themes.

- To evaluate the theories according to their coherence and comprehensiveness.

 Now please read Chapter 4, 'Living in the After-life: Knowledge and Social Change' and then return to this point in the workbook.

4.1 Narrative strand: models of social change

Each of the models which are outlined in Chapter 4 has a different view of the kind of social change which has taken place (or is still happening) and a different interpretation of the role played by *knowledge and knowing* in relation to that change. We will be going through some of the key features of the three models, but first a note about models and the use of social science language.

A note about models. One way in which social scientists try to explain their ideas is by building simplified 'models' of society (or parts of society) which describe and emphasize those features and interrelationships that they consider to be most important. These aren't physical models, of course, but their purpose can be compared with that of a diagram of how a car engine works or the sort of moving model that you might find in the Science Museum demonstrating the workings of some natural system. The difference is that whereas those models are representations of how things actually are, social science models are representations of how theorists *think* things work. And whereas we can all agree on how a motor car works, social scientists certainly don't agree with one another about the motive force in society.

A note about language and definitions. When writing about theories social scientists often use sociological terms in a way that can seem jargonistic and off-putting. Labels such as 'industrial' and 'post-industrial', 'Fordist' and 'post-Fordist', 'modern' and 'post-modern' serve as shorthand for complex ideas and are not susceptible to easy definition. (For example, the whole of Section 2.1 is taken up with explaining the first of these pairs.) Part of the process of studying the social sciences involves gradually learning what at first feels like a foreign language. We hope that after reading this chapter you will at least be more comfortable with the terms and able to use them appropriately – even if they don't exactly trip off the tongue!

You may already have been building up a glossary of terms used in the course. This is useful in helping you to come to grips with difficult ideas and also as a point of reference for you to use when you are writing your TMAs. Chapter 4 contains a number of words and concepts which may be unfamiliar to you, ranging from the broad concepts represented by the three models themselves to single words such as *epistemology*. Each of the sections dealing with the models has an activity at the end to test your understanding, but no single definition. **If you haven't yet completed Activities 4.1–4.3 please do so now.** Then have a go at the activity below.

WORKBOOK ACTIVITY 4.1

Define the terms below *using your own words* and in no more than three sentences each. (We're feeling generous today!)

The knowledge society

The fragmented society

The risk society

COMMENT

'Unfair!' we hear you cry. 'If it takes the author pages and pages how do you expect us to do it in three sentences?' But that's the point of the activities. We know that many students feel that they are a nuisance and get in the way of the 'real' work, but in fact they *are* the real work – the way in which you actually engage with the material rather than just read it. Having filled in the grids for the three models you should be able to extract from them the key features of each which need to be included in a definition.

We have cheated and used Table 4.1 in Section 5 to construct the following definition of the *risk society*:

THE RISK SOCIETY

A model of social change which characterizes contemporary (especially Western) society as shifting from a low-risk social, economic and political order in which security was related to class position and a minimum safety-net was guaranteed by the state to one in which risk is widespread and unavoidable (regardless of class), manufacturing industry is in decline, political systems have fallen apart, trust in experts has collapsed, and the state is no longer willing or able to provide services and universal social security.

All in one sentence! (OK – we admit it's rather a long one.)

"'Be careful'! All you can tell me is 'be careful'?"

The risk society

In addition to the three models themselves, the chapter is full of concepts which need defining and adding to your glossary list. Some of these are defined in marginal notes but others only appear in the text – some with a definition and some not.

WORKBOOK ACTIVITY 4.2

1   Make a list of the concepts and definitions given in the margins of Chapter 4 making a note of the models/context in which the concepts are used.

2   Add a further list of definitions of concepts used in the chapter which you think will be useful when you come to write your TMA.

COMMENT

Some of the marginal notes are just factual; for example, the explanations of *OPEC* and the *Bretton Woods system*, which are referred to in the discussion of the French *Regulationist* theory of social change (sometimes known as 'cyclical' theory or, more colloquially, as 'boom and bust'). But even words such as *professionals*, which are seemingly straightforward, need to be put in context. Professionals may also be called experts and, as you know, the role of experts is an important feature in the knowledge and knowing narrative theme as well as in the three models of social change discussed in Chapter 4.

As well as the words and concepts which appear in the marginal notes we listed the following.

Page number	
122	Post-industrial
123	Communications revolution
127	Knowledge worker
127	Knowledge entrepreneur
129	Regulationists
130	Fordist
131	Post-Fordism
132	Post-modernism
133	The Enlightenment
133	Representation
134	Epistemological

You may well have others. We're not going to offer you our definitions this time. The important thing is that *you* are happy that you understand what something means and can use concepts with confidence.

In the next section of the workbook we will be looking at how the three models relate to the course themes.

4.2 Using the course themes

Each of the models has a different emphasis on the themes of *knowledge and knowing, structure and agency* and *uncertainty and diversity*.

WORKBOOK ACTIVITY 4.3

Compare the three models summarized in Table 4.1 and then summarize their approaches to the course themes using the grid below.

	Knowledge society	Fragmented society	Risk society
Knowledge and knowing			

	Knowledge society	Fragmented society	Risk society
Structure and agency			
Uncertainty and diversity			

COMMENT _____

You probably found that some parts of the grid were quite easy to complete but that others needed hard work – for example, it is obvious that the model of the risk society has a lot to say about the *uncertainty and diversity* theme and the model of the knowledge society makes *knowledge and knowing* central to its ideas about social change. But you also need to examine how the fragmented society model fits in with the themes and the other two models, and compare how each deals with *structure and agency.*

In the past theories of social change have tended to emphasize the importance of structure. Marx, for example, saw society as being structured into dominant and subordinate classes on the basis of the predominant form of economic production. Change occurred when economic development led to changes in the mode of production, prompting a subordinate class to challenge the power of the dominant class and eventually to replace it. In this model the agents of change are social classes produced by the economic structure of society and the change which occurs is one in which society is *re*-structured in line with the new economic configuration.

If we look at the 'Forces of change' row in Table 4.1 we can see that structural changes in the economy feature very strongly in both the knowledge society and the fragmented society models and, whereas both tend to suggest that these will bring looser, more diverse forms of organization than was the case in the industrial or 'modern' period, there is no suggestion that social and economic structures will wither away or lose their importance. The risk society thesis is more ambiguous. If its analysis is taken at its most extreme it would seem to imply a world in which all social structures have been destroyed and we are all solely responsible for our own security and prosperity; a world in which, in Mrs Thatcher's famous phrase, there is no society, only individuals and their families.

You can compare your own response to this activity with the completed grid at the end of the workbook (p.74).

_____

4.3 Analytical strand: evaluating the theories

Having set out the main elements of the three models the remainder of Chapter 4 takes you through how to evaluate each in terms of coherence (covering conceptual clarity, logical reasoning and unsustainable assumptions) and comprehensiveness, and then draws some conclusions about the political and ideological aspects of different models of social change. This is very clearly set out but in order for you to learn how to do something similar you really need to practice pulling the ideas together and evaluating them yourself.

WORKBOOK ACTIVITY 4.4

1   Summarize the key claims of the three models in relation to knowledge and social change.

2   Evaluate these claims using the grid overleaf.

COMMENT _____

The work of actually evaluating the models according to their coherence and comprehensiveness has already been done for you in Chapter 4 so all you need to do is to plot these on the grid.

Our list of key claims was as follows.

Knowledge society

1   Theoretical knowledge, applied science, marketing knowledge, and technologies of communication and information processing have become the key assets in the economy.

"A muse! Are you IBM-compatible?"

The knowledge society

	Conceptual clarity	Logical reasoning
Knowledge society		
Fragmented society		
Risk society		

Unsustainable assumptions

Comprehensiveness

2   This has led to the transformation of corporate structures and labour markets and will increasingly determine the character of society, politics and culture.

3   Social groups that produce, possess and use these forms of knowledge will be the most politically powerful.

Fragmented society

1   The pursuit of profit remains the driving force of social change and new technologies of communication and information have been a means to that end.

2   The role of economic experts has declined because the economic conditions under which they could practically operate have been transformed.

3   The same processes account for the declining authority of intellectuals.

Risk society

1   Widespread knowledge of contemporary risks and their potential consequences is the main driving force in changing the agenda of politics.

2   Knowledge of these risks continually undermines the claims and authority of experts.

In addition to evaluating the arguments identified by looking at coherence and comprehensiveness Chapter 4 emphasizes that we also need to take into account the normative aspects of the different models. As Chapter 3 pointed out, in relation to green alternatives, theories are not just different descriptions of how the theorists think society works – they also incorporate ideological prescriptions about what is good and bad and what *ought* to happen. Thus, although we can try to compare and evaluate our models in an objective manner our choice between them will depend as much on where we are coming from and where we want to go to as on what we can reliably 'know'.

You might worry that this means we can't evaluate the three models at all, but we don't think that that is so. As long as we are *aware* of the ideological aspects of theories and models we can put those into the equation along with everything else.

WORKBOOK ACTIVITY 4.5

We have identified the political and normative arguments incorporated in each of the three models on the grid below. Add a further row to the grid summarizing the main forms of political response which each model suggests.

	Knowledge society	Fragmented society	Risk society
Main political ideologies embedded in theory	Liberalism	Social democracy Marxism	Environmentalism
Normative and political concerns about social change	Cultural fragmentation Social exclusion Declining national competitiveness	New forms of inequality Marginalization Crises of identity, meaninglessness	Global environmental catastrophe Breakdown of legitimate politics
Main forms of political response to social change			

C O M M E N T

Our guess is that you are getting a bit fed up with grids by now! But setting things out like this is not only a form of note taking that allows you to identify the key points in each of the arguments it also helps you to *compare* different approaches. In this case we can see that although some of the normative and political concerns about social change are common to all three models (for example, social exclusion, marginalization and the breakdown of democratic politics) the ideological assumptions which lie behind them are different. It follows from this that the political agenda for change is also different.

If you check your response to the activity against the completed grid at the back of the workbook (p.75) we're sure you will find that, although you may not have the same wording, the gist of what you have written is similar and that the biggest contrast is between the two models which are based largely on 'mainstream' ideology (the knowledge society and the fragmented society) and the risk society, which is based on environmentalism. This would seem to bear out the argument of Chapter 3 that mainstream ideologies have failed, but remember that that is a *normative* argument – in other words, it is a *judgement*, not a fact.

That brings us full circle, back to the question of the nature of knowledge and how we can know anything. What Section 6 in Chapter 4 points out is that it is not possible to reach a definitive conclusion on these matters. It never has been, the difference is that now more and more people are aware of how uncertain our knowledge is.

5 REFLECTION AND CONSOLIDATION

As usual you now have the opportunity to consolidate and reflect on your work in this block and complete the TMA question. The Afterword to Book 5 and Side B of Audio-cassette 9 are designed to help you to do this and you should also draw on TV 05.

 Pause now to read the Afterword to Book 5, listen to Side B of Audio-cassette 9 and read the associated notes. Also watch TV 05 around this time (depending on broadcast schedules) and read the associated notes.

Then return to this point in the workbook.

Throughout the course we can trace a narrative strand of the *knowledge and knowing* theme and an analytical strand. The narrative aspect of the theme deals with the diversity of different forms of knowledge and how alternative systems have developed to challenge old orthodoxies and bring about social change. It argues that in a variety of different spheres of society, including medicine and the natural sciences, management of the environment, the family, the world of work, and relations between states, dominant forms of knowledge which were previously controlled by experts and institutions have been challenged by alternative systems.

The analytical strand looks at the social sciences as a particular form of knowledge in order to examine how changes in knowledge come about. This involves analysing the process of how we come to 'know' something, how social scientists gather information and evidence, and how they construct arguments and explanations. As we noted in the introduction to the workbook, synthesis and integration are the final elements in the *circuit of knowledge* whereby aspects of different competing and complementary theories are absorbed, modified and reworked to produce new, and it is hoped more illuminating, ideas and explanations.

In order to complete the circuit we need to go through two separate stages: first we need to bring together (*synthesize*) the different things which have been said about *knowledge and knowing* throughout the block and to sum them up. Then we need to compare and consider the implications of the arguments which have been put forward, and to *integrate* those aspects of each argument to help us develop a new explanation which takes these implications into account and helps us to understand more about the process of studying society and tackling the problems which we identify. In this section we will be concentrating on helping you to synthesize the narrative and the analytical aspects of the knowledge and knowing theme. The *Mid Course Review* has already summarized the development of the theme in the Introductory Block and Blocks 1–3 in Table 3 (p.37) and Figure 3 (p.38). To complete the table we have added the narrative and analytical strands introduced in Blocks 4 and 5.

TABLE 2   Knowledge and knowing in DD100 (part of this table is Table 3 in the *Mid Course Review*)

Course material	Knowledge and knowing: analytical strand	Knowledge and knowing: narrative strand
Introductory Chapter	Section 3: on quantitative and qualitative evidence. Section 5.1: overview.	
Workbook 1	Sections 1–4: on concepts, theories and explanations. Section 1.4: introduction to the circuit of knowledge.	
Study Skills Supplement 1: Reading Visual Images	Using photographs as a source of evidence.	
Workbook 2	Using evidence in the social sciences.	
Book 2, Chapter 2		Contested medical knowledges.
Book 2, Chapter 4		Contested understandings of natural disasters and environmental risks.
Workbook 3	Sections 1–4: using theories in the social sciences.	
Book 3, Chapters 2–4		Role of political ideologies in social science and their impact on the social world.
Book 3, Chapters 2 and 3	Comparisons of political ideologies on specific topics. Chapter 2: feminism and conservatism on the family. Chapter 3: liberalism and social democracy on the labour market.	
Study Skills Supplement 2: Reading Evidence	Reading evidence.	
Workbook 4	Section 1.2: Globalization – concepts and evidence. Section 2.2: Examining the coherence of an argument. Section 2.3: Reading quantitative and diagrammatic evidence. Section 3.3: Practice with numbers. Section 3.4: An evaluation of the traditionalist view of globalization. Section 4.2: Evaluating the transformationalist argument. Section 5.1: Evaluation revisited.	Sections 1.2, 1.3, 2.4, 3.2, 4.1 and 5.2.

Course material	Knowledge and knowing: analytical strand	Knowledge and knowing: narrative strand
Book 4, Chapter 1	Section 5: measuring globalization, looking for evidence.	Section 4: the big debates.
Book 4, Chapter 3	Sections 4 and 5: how to measure the extent of globalization.	
Workbook 5	Introduction: knowledge and knowing, analytical strand. Section 1.2: scientific and social scientific knowledge. Section 2.3: investigating religion. Section 3.3: ideology and the circuit of knowledge. Section 4.3: evaluating the theories. Section 5: Reflection and consolidation.	Introduction: knowledge and knowing, narrative strand. Section 1.1: the social production of knowledge. Section 2.1: the status of religious knowledge. Section 3.1: knowledge, ideology and the environment. Section 4.1: models of social change.
Book 5, Introduction		What is knowledge?
Book 5, Chapter 1	Section 2.1: proof and the construction of scientific debate. Section 3: science and social science ways of thinking.	Section 2: knowledge, medicine and science. Section 4: Who are the experts? Section 5: science and society.
Book 5, Chapter 2	Section 2.2: methods and finding out. Sections 3–6: different kinds of evidence about religious belief.	Sections 3–6: secularization and gender, ethnicity and New Age beliefs.
Book 5, Chapter 3	Section 5: evaluating political ideologies.	Section 1: political ideologies. Section 4: the challenge of green thinking.
Book 5, Chapter 4	Section 5: evaluating the theories.	Sections 1–6: knowledge and social change.
Book 5, Afterword	Social change and the social sciences.	Expert and elite knowledges, knowledge and social change.
Audio-cassette 9		Side B: knowledge and social change.

You can't say we don't help you! You now have a map of the knowledge and knowing theme that you can use to help you to tackle TMA 05 and can refer back to when it comes to TMA 06. But remember, a map is just a one-dimensional version of where you have been. If you haven't been looking around and paying attention as we have gone along you may still end up getting lost.

6 ASSESSING BLOCK 5

TMA 05 aims to help you to pull together the material on knowledge and knowing that you have studied in this block and to practice the key skill for the block – the ability to **synthesize and integrate** arguments and evidence.

Before starting on TMA 05 we want you to look at the practice TMA and student notes below (a real TMA used in 2000). Ask yourself the questions that follow and make a plan which identifies the structure of your essay, your main argument and the material from Block 5 which you would use. Then look at our comments and check your plan against the tutors' marking notes at the back of the workbook.

Practice TMA

In approximately 1,500 words, examine the ways in which knowledge can be said to be *socially produced* and how this is related to social change. Illustrate your answer with arguments and evidence from two or more of the chapters in Book 5.

100 marks

Student notes

Note that you are asked to **relate** the idea of the social production of knowledge to that of social change and it is for this that you will earn most credit. Answers making relevant use of the course themes of structure and agency and uncertainty and diversity will also be rewarded. You will probably find it easier to structure your essay if you take a step by step approach to this, *first* examining the arguments about the social production of knowledge and *then* relating these to social change.

In constructing your answer you will find relevant material in all four of the chapters in Book 5. For example:

Chapter 1 introduces the idea that knowledge has an inevitable social aspect and uses the example of the history of the development of medical science to illustrate arguments about subjectivity, objectivity and different ways in which it has been argued that knowledge is socially produced.

Chapter 2 is concerned with how religious knowledge is socially constructed, whether religion has been replaced by scientific knowledge or has simply changed its social basis, how different definitions of religion can influence our conclusions, and how social change has influenced religious belief.

Chapter 3 explains the way that political ideologies are shaped by existing institutions and social interrelationships, how these dictate our response to the environment and how they are influenced by social change.

Chapter 4 explores different ideas about the relationship between knowledge and social change.

Other useful material can be found in Audio-cassette 9, Side B and TV 05 and associated notes.

Planning your essay

Refer back to the essay planning advice in *Workbook 2* and *Workbook 4* and to your tutor's feedback on the essay that you wrote for TMA 04.

Workbook 4 suggests that you ask yourself the following questions before starting to plan the essay:

- What type of question is it?
- What length of answer is required?
- Are there any other specific requirements?
- What is the central subject matter?
- What are the key arguments/conflicting theories on offer?
- Where will I locate my main sources of evidence?
- What will my basic conclusion be?
- How will I structure my answer?

Take a moment to think about your own answers to these questions before consulting my comments below which apply the questions to this practice TMA.

Comments

What type of question is it? The key words in the question are 'examine' and 'illustrate'. 'Examine' entails looking at different aspects and weighing them up. 'Illustrate' means using concrete examples taken from the text as **evidence** to back up the points you are making. You don't have to go through them all in great detail one by one. You need to pick out the key points of each which relate to the question (that is the *synthesis* part of your answer) and then *integrate* those aspects which appear strongest into your own argument and conclusion.

What length of answer is required? We give word limits not because we want you to become obsessed with counting every single word but because we want you to develop the skill of selecting and summarizing appropriate material and expressing an argument concisely. If you go drastically over length, you can expect to be penalized because of your lack of focus and failure to be succinct. But remember that **what** you write is more important than the precise number of words!

Are there any other specific requirements? You have to give examples from two or more chapters. This doesn't mean that you must illustrate every single point in this way but that during the course of the essay you should show your knowledge of the chapters through your use of examples. *Don't forget to provide page references.*

What is the central subject matter? The question is specifically about (i) the social production of knowledge and (ii) the relationship between this and social change. The social production of knowledge is dealt with in every chapter but we don't want lengthy chapter summaries. Pick out those key arguments and examples which relate to the discussion of social change in Chapter 4.

What are the key arguments/conflicting theories on offer? Read the student notes to see if they give you any advice. If they do, don't ignore it! If they don't, go back to your notes or to the chapter summaries and identify and examine those arguments which relate to the question.

Where will I locate my main sources of evidence? Again, read the student notes. Don't forget to use other sources too (TV, audio tapes, etc.) and to refer to the course themes where these are relevant.

What will my basic conclusion be? Your conclusion should follow from your discussion. We want you to bring together the different arguments in the block, to pick out those which you find most relevant and to integrate them into your conclusion.

How will I structure my answer? Make a plan! The simplest way to structure an essay is to say what you are going to do, do it, then say what you have done. When you are building onto this framework you might use some of the chapters as a model (check back on Chapter 3, for example). Remember to:

- **Identify** different ways in which knowledge is socially produced and different arguments about social change.

- **Consider** the different arguments, using examples.

- **Discuss** the interpretation of the evidence and its strengths and weaknesses.

- **Reach a conclusion, stating your reasons**.

This is intended to help you so please give it a go before comparing your plan with the tutor notes at the back of the workbook (pp.76–8). Once you have done that it is on to TMA 05 proper and then on to the final block, Block 6. If you have got this far you've nearly made it. Nothing can stop you now!

 Now turn to the *Assignments Booklet* for TMA 05.

COMMENT ON WORKBOOK
ACTIVITY 1.2

You could have used the summaries at the end of each section but we
constructed the grid below without them in order to try to use our own
words. (It's worth looking at the summaries now, however.)

	Argument	Examples/evidence
Section 2	There is a difference between religious and common-sense knowledge and 'scientific' knowledge; scientific knowledge has come to the fore since the seventeenth century.	The basis of medical knowledge has changed from folk/religious/magical to scientific; the body of medical knowledge and medical training has also changed.
	Expert knowledge develops within a specific community and institutional framework which influences the direction of change and bestows authority on it.	Medical science in the UK developed in the context of the scientific Royal Society and was given authority by the status of the Society and its members; women were excluded.
	The development of institutionalized scientific knowledge privileged objectivity over subjectivity and the rational over the emotional.	Medical science developed using verifiable scientific methodologies; common-sense knowledge and women's knowledge were devalued.
	Scientific methodology aims to produce knowledge that is known to be true because it is subject to objective proof; theories which cannot be scientifically verified are declared to be false; double-blind studies are used to eliminate subjective bias.	Forms of medicine such as homeopathy have been rejected by the medical establishment because they have not been scientifically verified and have not been tested using double-blind methodology.
	Different interest groups have a vested interest in different forms of knowledge.	Medical research is supported by drug companies but this has to pass the scrutiny of 'learned bodies' and scientific journals which impose their own strict criteria.
Section 3	The natural sciences claim to be entirely objective but the way in which science actually works is not so clear cut.	Example of Edmund Stone and the willow bark.

Argument	Examples/evidence
Scientific method is based on proving hypotheses by testing evidence.	
There are a number of different theories about how knowledge is produced which challenge the idea of scientific objectivity and emphasize social construction.	Doctors use diagnosis to prove that patients are ill. Doctors accept that diagnosis is not an exact science and employ common-sense as well as scientific knowledge.
Popper: It is only possible to prove a negative not a positive. Scientists should seek to falsify theories not verify them.	
Kuhn: science is interconnected with social change. Scientists develop sets of assumptions, laws and methods (paradigms) which are often replaced by new ones; scientific knowledge develops in fits and starts according to its social context.	The Royal Society is the product of the scientific revolution which followed the English Civil War
Foucault: Knowledge is produced through the language and practices used to interpret different phenomena and is therefore related to culture and power; knowledge and power are inextricably linked.	Illness is 'invented' and classified according to the dominant discourse of the time, medical diagnosis is historically and culturally specific, e.g. in relation to 'humours', 'hysteria', M.E.
Fox Keller: Knowledge is not gender neutral; it is gendered by the social structures through which it is produced.	The (male) medical establishment controls what is 'counted' as illness. Women are a majority in the NHS but not in the higher echelons because they were historically excluded from universities and medical guilds and could not, therefore, practice medicine.

	Argument	Examples/evidence
Section 4	Our definition of Knowledge is influenced by the way in which it is represented. There are competing definitions. Whether or not the dominant definition changes depends on the authority of those doing the representing. In the twentieth century the power of the media has increased. This may be used by existing sources of authority in support of the existing orthodoxy or it may be used to support new forms of Knowledge which challenge that orthodoxy.	SIDS case study.
	Social and cultural assumptions (e.g. about gender) influence theories and privilege expert Knowledge over other forms.	Cultural assumptions about motherhood obscured other explanations for SIDS and the gender hierarchy devalued the evidence of traditional female Knowledge.
Section 5	Knowledge is applied and passed on through practices which acquire their own traditions and social institutions.	Traditionally medical practice was embodied in the medical profession, governed by the Hippocratic oath and a system of craft apprenticeship which was limited to men. Today the scientific profession and the academic publishing system perform a similar role in reinforcing existing practices and making dissent difficult.
	Knowledge and power are interrelated. Access to Knowledge can be restricted in the interests of particular social groups. Knowledge can be used for political ends.	Case study on smoking and health.

COMMENT ON WORKBOOK
ACTIVITY 4.3 _____

We have taken relevant points from Figures 4.3–4.6 and plotted them on the
grid as shown below.

	Knowledge society	Fragmented society	Risk society
Knowledge and knowing	Society is characterized by the dominant form of knowledge. There has been an explosion of scientific research and new technology and a shift from an industrial economy to a knowledge economy. Knowledge is the key to competitiveness; skilled and knowledgeable labour is very important.	Fordist technology is replaced by new technologies and the information revolution. There is a shift to post-Fordism and a decline in the power of the nation-state and economic experts.	Increased complexity and interrelatedness makes risks unknowable and unmanageable. Legitimacy of experts undermined, politics dominated by contestation of meaning and expertise.
Structure and agency	Global economics and culture are more important than national structures. Large hierarchical corporations are replaced by more flexible organizations capable of adapting to rapid change. There is a rebalancing of politics and class structures become less important.	There is a restructuring of the global economy on neo-liberal lines. Market structures become more important than national governments. There is a collapse of the welfare state and risk is individualized.	Old structures (e.g. class and nation) are unable to manage increasing risks and become irrelevant.
Uncertainty and diversity	Society is culturally more diverse. Expansion of knowledge decreases risk and uncertainty.	There is a fragmentation of politics, economics and culture; a crisis of reason/science; and an increase in political conflicts.	Society is dominated by new forms of risk that have no spatial, social or temporal limits. There is increased risk of global catastrophe and old forms of risk management (e.g. legal, collective) are no longer viable.

COMMENT ON WORKBOOK ACTIVITY 4.5

	Knowledge society	Fragmented society	Risk society
Main forms of political response to social change	Reorientation of political priorities in response to globalization. Increased responsiveness to electorates.	Change from class-based politics to interest-based politics. Growth of regionalism and of new oppositional movements.	Need for risk management leads to a growth in the influence of scientists and expert bodies. Alternative political parties develop addressing environmental risks (e.g. the Green Party). More power given to international bodies.

COMMENT ON BLOCK 5 SAMPLE ESSAY QUESTION

Content

The following notes on possible content are based on the guidance given to tutors for marking this question.

The assignment requires students to identify and bring together arguments and evidence about the social production of knowledge from different places in the block and then to relate these to the concept of social change. The key skills here are synthesis and integration. Answers should be in the from of a structured essay, drawing on appropriate theories, evidence and terminology from the sources below and reaching a reasoned and well-supported conclusion.

Key concepts

Knowledge, objectivity, subjectivity, discourse, paradigm, ideology, social construction, social change, risk, uncertainty, post-modernism.

Key sources

Relevant arguments and examples can be used from any of the four chapters. These are summarized below. We do *not* expect students to use them all!

Chapter 1

Section 1 introduces the idea that knowledge takes more than one form. It has an inevitable social aspect because it is communicated and conveyed socially. For example, both common-sense knowledge and medical knowledge have social origins.

Section 2 uses the example of the development of medical science and the roles of the Royal Society and the dissemination of ideas through a social process of academic journals and peer review.

Section 3 outlines the critique of the idea of scientific objectivity by the social constructionist approach.

Section 4 illustrates the influence of the media in representing ideas and the part played by cultural factors in determining which theories are accepted.

Section 5 makes the point that scientists are not passive observers but control knowledge for particular ends. The scientific establishment behaves as a social institution in its own right, shaping the knowledge agents that work within it.

Chapter 2

Section 1 outlines the concern of the chapter with how religious knowledge is socially constructed and whether religion has been replaced by scientific knowledge or has simply changed its social basis.

Section 2 discusses the substantive and functional definitions of religion. It argues that the choice of definition will influence whether you think religion is declining or not and that the interpretative approach allows for different meanings.

Section 3 uses statistics on belief to show that there are differences between different societies and that belief is stronger where more relevant to the social and cultural situation, e.g. in Northern Ireland where there are opposing collective identities or the USA where there have been successive waves of immigrants.

Sections 4 and 5 show how gender and ethnicity influence belief. Religion reflects patriarchal social structures, represents common culture and security and may be a form of identity.

Section 6 argues that new circumstances may lead to a redefinition of religion, e.g. ecologism etc. may be a response to social change such as modernization, globalization and secularization. New Age beliefs may offer new moral meanings.

Chapter 3

Section 1 explains that political ideologies are maps of the social world that aim to tell us how that world works; networks of concepts linked by history and culture formed by abstracting from social life, grounded in social relations and practices. They are linked to social change because they are prescriptive, help to shape understanding and actions, and to alter society.

Section 2 argues that knowledge about the environment is uncertain because science is historically and culturally specific and therefore inadequate to understand complex environmental problems or the environmental implications of economic and other social activity. Knowledge and ideology are territorially bounded – politics makes us view people as separate communities not part of the same world and ideologies fail to recognize natural limits or the natural and social consequences of scientific actions. Nature is no longer separate from society but shaped by it. There is a complex interaction and increasing uncertainty – leading to transition from modern industrial to late modern risk society.

Section 3 describes the response of mainstream ideologies as being shaped by existing institutions and familiar questions, variables and methods; e.g. market economics or managed market, property rights, nation-state, etc.

Section 4 summarizes the ecological perspective, which argues that mainstream perspectives are the products of industrialism and materialism but points out that this is also socially produced. Human beings inevitably interact with the environment and are part of nature and it has been argued that the environmental paradigm is also anthropocentric and rests on ideas about the relationship between man and nature and how this influences society. The definition of nature includes socially generated attitudes and interests, scientific, spiritual or evaluative.

Section 5 relates the discussion to social change. Mainstream ideologies merely adapt their approach to take account of environmental problems. Greens seek to break with previous assumptions but which map is the most use?

Chapter 4

Section 1 argues that changes in knowledge produce social change.

Section 2 outlines the theory of the knowledge society and how this has its origins in Bell's theory of post-industrial society. The knowledge society is distinguished by a concern with how knowledge is produced and used in the economy. It is the main source of innovation, productivity and competitiveness, and social and cultural results will flow from this.

Section 3 traces the origins of the theory of the fragmented society, which argues that the post-war growth of new knowledge-intensive industry, rapid growth and deregulation has led to the fragmentation of industry and society.

Section 4 outlines the theory of the risk society, which sees the growth in our knowledge of the environment as undermining old forms of social organization and requiring new ones.

Audio-cassette 9

Side B contains relevant discussion.

TV 05

Explores diversity of knowledge and the role of experts in modern parenting.

REFERENCE

Durkheim, E. (1912/1965) *The Elementary Forms of the Religious Life* (trans. J.W. Swain), New York, Free Press.

80

WORKBOOK 5

ACKNOWLEDGEMENTS

Grateful acknowledgement is made to the following sources for permission to reproduce material in this workbook.

Text

Devlin, K. (1999) 'Where Darwin is a dirty word', *Guardian Higher*, 14 September 1999, © Keith Devlin, 1999.

Cartoons

p.12: © Larry. Reproduced with permission of Punch Ltd; p.34: © Raymonde. Reproduced with permission of Punch Ltd; pp.44 and 54: © Sidney Harris; p.47: © Rolf Henn; p.59: © Schwadron. Reproduced with permission of Punch Ltd.

Cover

Image copyright © 1996 PhotoDisc, Inc.

STUDY SKILLS INDEX